# The

# Constitution

# of the

# United States

CHRISTINE TAYLOR-BUTLER

**Children's Press®**
An Imprint of Scholastic Inc.
New York  Toronto  London  Auckland  Sydney
Mexico City  New Delhi  Hong Kong
Danbury, Connecticut

**Content Consultant**

David R. Smith, PhD

Academic Adviser and

Adjunct Assistant Professor of History

University of Michigan–Ann Arbor


**Reading Consultant**

Cecilia Minden-Cupp, PhD

Early Literacy Consultant and Author


Library of Congress Cataloging-in-Publication Data

Taylor-Butler, Christine.
The Constitution / by Christine Taylor-Butler.
    p. cm.—(A true book)
Includes bibliographical references and index.
ISBN-13: 978-0-531-12629-5 (lib. bdg.)        978-0-531-14779-5 (pbk.)
ISBN-10: 0-531-12629-3 (lib. bdg.)        0-531-14779-7 (pbk.)
1. United States. Constitution—Juvenile literature. 2. United States—Politics and government—
1775-1783—Juvenile literature. 3. United States—Politics and government—1783-1789—Juvenile
literature. 4. Constitutional history—United States—Juvenile literature. I. Title. II. Series.
E303.T35 2008
973.4—dc22                        2007005156

# Find the Truth!

**Everything** you are about to read is true *except* for one of the sentences on this page.

Which one is **TRUE**?

T or F    The Constitution is made up of all the laws of the United States.

T or F    The Constitution created today's U.S. government.

Find the answer in this book.

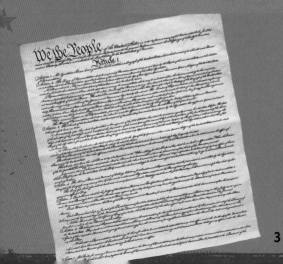

3

# Contents

## THE BIG TRUTH!

## Meet Five Framers of the Constitution

# We the People

of the United States, in order to form a more perfect Union, establish Justice, insure domestic Tranquility, provide for the common defence, promote the general Welfare, and secure the Blessings of Liberty to ourselves and our Posterity, do ordain and establish this Constitution for the United States of America.

## Article. I.

Section. 1. All legislative Powers herein granted shall be vested in a Congress of the United States, which shall consist of a Senate and House of Representatives.

Section. 2. The House of Representatives shall be composed of Members chosen every second Year by the People of the several States, and the Electors in each State shall have the Qualifications requisite for Electors of the most numerous Branch of the State Legislature.

No Person shall be a Representative who shall not have attained to the Age of twenty five Years, and been seven Years a Citizen of the United States, and who shall not, when elected, be an Inhabitant of that State in which he shall be chosen.

Representatives and direct Taxes shall be apportioned among the several States which may be included within this Union, according to their respective Numbers, which shall be determined by adding to the whole Number of free Persons, including those bound to Service for a Term of Years, and excluding Indians not taxed, three fifths of all other Persons. The actual Enumeration shall be made within three Years after the first Meeting of the Congress of the United States, and within every subsequent Term of ten Years, in such Manner as they shall by Law direct. The Number of Representatives shall not exceed one for every thirty Thousand, but each State shall have at Least one Representative; and until such enumeration shall be made, the State of New Hampshire shall be entitled to chuse three, Massachusetts eight, Rhode Island and Providence Plantations one, Connecticut five, New York six, New Jersey four, Pennsylvania eight, Delaware one, Maryland six, Virginia ten, North Carolina five, South Carolina five, and Georgia three.

When vacancies happen in the Representation from any State, the Executive Authority thereof shall issue Writs of Election to fill such Vacancies.

The House of Representatives shall chuse their Speaker and other Officers; and shall have the sole Power of Impeachment.

Section. 3. The Senate of the United States shall be composed of two Senators from each State, chosen by the Legislature thereof for six Years; and each Senator shall have one Vote.

Immediately after they shall be assembled in Consequence of the first Election, they shall be divided as equally as may be into three Classes. The Seats of the Senators of the first Class shall be vacated at the Expiration of the second Year, of the second Class at the Expiration of the fourth Year, and of the third Class at the Expiration of the sixth Year, so that one third may be chosen every second Year; and if Vacancies happen by Resignation, or otherwise, during the Recess of the Legislature of any State, the Executive thereof may make temporary Appointments until the next Meeting of the Legislature, which shall then fill such Vacancies.

No Person shall be a Senator who shall not have attained to the Age of thirty Years, and been nine Years a Citizen of the United States, and who shall not, when elected, be an Inhabitant of that State for which he shall be chosen.

The Vice President of the United States shall be President of the Senate, but shall have no Vote, unless they be equally divided.

The Senate shall chuse their other Officers, and also a President pro tempore, in the Absence of the Vice President, or when he shall exercise the Office of President of the United States.

The Senate shall have the sole Power to try all Impeachments. When sitting for that Purpose, they shall be on Oath or Affirmation. When the President of the United States is tried, the Chief Justice shall preside: And no Person shall be convicted without the Concurrence of two thirds of the Members present.

Judgment in Cases of Impeachment shall not extend further than to removal from Office, and disqualification to hold and enjoy any Office of honor, Trust or Profit under the United States: but the Party convicted shall nevertheless be liable and subject to Indictment, Trial, Judgment and Punishment, according to Law.

Section. 4. The Times, Places and Manner of holding Elections for Senators and Representatives, shall be prescribed in each State by the Legislature thereof; but the Congress may at any time by Law make or alter such Regulations, except as to the Places of chusing Senators.

The Congress shall assemble at least once in every Year, and such Meeting shall be on the first Monday in December, unless they shall by Law appoint a different Day.

Section. 5. Each House shall be the Judge of the Elections, Returns and Qualifications of its own Members, and a Majority of each shall constitute a Quorum to do Business; but a smaller Number may adjourn from day to day, and may be authorized to compel the Attendance of absent Members, in such Manner, and under such Penalties as each House may provide.

Each House may determine the Rules of its Proceedings, punish its Members for disorderly Behaviour, and, with the Concurrence of two thirds, expel a Member.

Each House shall keep a Journal of its Proceedings, and from time to time publish the same, excepting such Parts as may in their Judgment require Secrecy; and the Yeas and Nays of the Members of either House on any question shall, at the Desire of one fifth of those Present, be entered on the Journal.

Neither House, during the Session of Congress, shall, without the Consent of the other, adjourn for more than three days, nor to any other Place than that in which the two Houses shall be sitting.

Section. 6. The Senators and Representatives shall receive a Compensation for their Services, to be ascertained by Law, and paid out of the Treasury of the United States. They shall in all Cases, except Treason, Felony and Breach of the Peace, be privileged from Arrest during their Attendance at the Session of their respective Houses, and in going to and returning from the same; and for any Speech or Debate in either House, they shall not be questioned in any other Place.

No Senator or Representative shall, during the Time for which he was elected, be appointed to any civil Office under the Authority of the United States, which shall have been created, or the Emoluments whereof shall have been encreased during such time; and no Person holding any Office under the United States, shall be a Member of either House during his Continuance in Office.

Section. 7. All Bills for raising Revenue shall originate in the House of Representatives; but the Senate may propose or concur with Amendments as on other Bills.

Every Bill which shall have passed the House of Representatives and the Senate, shall, before it become a Law, be presented to the President of the

**The original Constitution is on display at the National Archives in Washington, D.C.**

# CHAPTER 1

# What Is a Constitution?

The United States has the oldest written constitution in the world.

A **constitution** is a powerful piece of paper. It can create a government where there was none. And it says what that government can and can't do. The Constitution of the United States is more than 200 years old. It still guides our country today.

# Creating a Government

The Constitution created a **federal** government. That's a national government that shares power with a group of smaller governments, such as states.

The U.S. federal government has many powers. It can pass laws. It can collect taxes. It can also form a military. People in all states must follow the laws passed by the federal government. But states have the power to pass their own laws.

The United States had formed a military by 1794, when the army defeated a group of Native Americans in the Battle of Fallen Timbers.

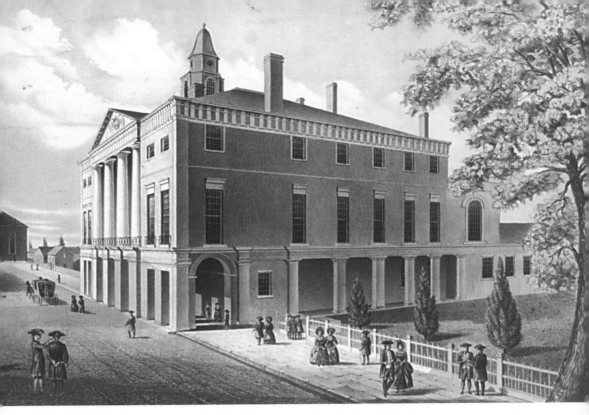

Federal Hall, in New York City, housed the United States government before 1790. In that year, the capital moved to Philadelphia, Pennsylvania.

The Constitution set up three parts, or branches, of the government. It created the office of the president who is the leader of the country. It created a **congress** with the power to make laws. And it created a system of federal courts to try important cases.

In 1787, leaders at the Constitutional Convention decided on a government that still runs the United States today.

The leaders of the new nation had many problems to solve and arguments to settle. Should the federal government be weak or strong? Should big states have more power than small states? And who should be counted as a citizen? The Constitution answered all these questions. But getting it written wasn't easy.

# Who Needs a Constitution?

The country just didn't work right before the Constitution was passed in 1788. Here are some examples of the problems:

- The states wouldn't give money to the federal government. The government couldn't pay the army. Soldiers often just went home.

- The states made each other pay very high taxes on goods. It was hard to do business.

- Pirates caught American sailors and made them slaves. The United States had no navy to protect it.

**This illustration of pirates by N. C. Wyeth is from the book _Treasure Island_ by Robert Louis Stevenson.**

LAKE SUPERIOR

Marquette

NORTH

LAKE MICHIGAN

LAKE HURON

Joliet

TERRITORY

Ft. Wayne

WEST

Vincennes

St. Louis
Kaskaskia

Ohio R.

VIRGINIA

Organized in 1787

Memphis

SOUTH WEST

TERRITORY

Nashville

belonged to N.C. until 1790

River

TERRITORY

OF

MISSISSIPPI

Organized in 1802

Natchez

Mobile

Pensacola

Mobile

Orleans

MISSISSIPPI

Montreal

St. Lawrence

PROV.

VERMONT

N. HAMPSHIRE

Organized in 1791

NEW YORK

L. ONTARIO

Ft. Niagara

Albany

MASS.
Springfield

Hartford

CONN.

LAKE ERIE

PENNSYLVANIA

Pittsburg

Philadelphia

Ft. Necessity

LONG ISLAND

New York

NEW JERSEY

Trenton

Baltimore

MARYLAND

Potomac R.

Annapolis

Chesapeake B.

DEL.

Cape Mary
Delaware Bay

Cape Henlope

Richmond

Cape Charles
Cape Henry

Albemarle Sou

Raleigh

NORTH CAROLINA

Cape Hatte

C. Lookout

SOUTH
CAROLINA

Cape Fear

GEORGIA

Savannah R.

Charleston

Altamaha R.

Savannah

St. Augustine

FLORIDA

This map shows the
United States when
it first declared
independence.

12

# CHAPTER 2

# The Divided States of America

Benjamin Franklin suggested calling the new country "the United Colonies of North America."

The United States was not united at all when it was first formed in 1776. Leaders from the new 13 states fought about almost everything. Some even refused to go to meetings. How would the country ever come together? Could they agree on a set of rules to govern themselves?

The first battle of the Revolutionary War was fought in Lexington, Massachusetts. Eight colonists were killed, and nine others were wounded.

Some people wanted a government to lead all the states. Others didn't. The country was fighting the British in the **Revolutionary War**. People wanted freedom from the British government. Some feared that a strong U.S. government would take away too much of their freedom.

Each state sent **delegates**, or representatives, to Philadelphia, Pennsylvania. The delegates created a plan for a weak federal government known as the Articles of Confederation.

# The Country in Trouble

The war with Great Britain ended in 1783. The United States was now free! But the excitement didn't last long. The Articles of Confederation were causing big problems.

There was no easy way to resolve disputes between the states. The country did not have a national court system. To make or change a law, a **unanimous** vote of the states was needed. That meant every state had to agree. So nothing was getting done!

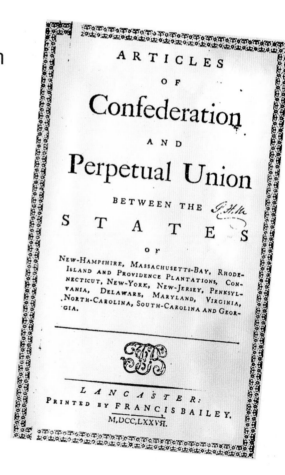

The Articles of Confederation were ratified on March 1, 1781. The plan created a very weak government.

# Money Problems

The new government didn't have any money. It had borrowed nearly $70 million from other countries to pay for the war. It couldn't collect taxes to pay its debt.

States had money problems, too. Massachusetts farmers rebelled against rising state taxes. The federal government had no army and few weapons to fight back. The fighting alarmed Americans. They worried that the new government couldn't keep the peace.

**A farmer named Daniel Shays led 1,500 men in a revolt against the Massachusetts government. This was called Shays's Rebellion.**

## Time to Do Something!

The leaders realized the Articles of Confederation didn't work. The United States was falling apart.

A leader from Virginia named James Madison wanted to help create a strong government. Madison thought about what would be best for his young

**James Madison spent a year reading about different governments before the Constitutional Convention.**

country. He was well-prepared for the large meeting, or convention. He arrived before anyone else, sat in the front row, and took detailed notes each day.

In 1809, James Madison became the fourth president of the United States.

# The Small Starter:
## William Paterson

(1745–1806) New Jersey

William Paterson stood up for the smaller states. Paterson wanted all the states to have the same power in Congress. His idea became the model for the U.S. Senate.

# The Writer:
## Gouverneur Morris

(1752–1816) Pennsylvania

Gouverneur Morris wrote most of the final draft of the Constitution. He wrote the document's most famous words: "We the People of the United States, in order to form a more perfect Union . . ."

# The Leader:
## George Washington

(1732–1799) Virginia

All the delegates agreed: George Washington would be president of the Constitutional Convention. Washington was the hero of the Revolutionary War. He inspired the delegates to work hard and trust one another.

# The Uniter:
## Benjamin Franklin

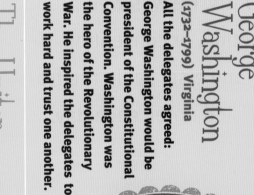

(1706–1790) Pennsylvania

Benjamin Franklin was the oldest member of the Constitutional Convention. Others listened to his ideas. He gave a powerful speech. He got the unhappy delegates to sign the Constitution.

18

# Meet Five Framers of the Constitution

A total of 55 delegates went to Philadelphia in the spring of 1787 to work on the Constitution. These five men played important roles.

### The Planner: James Madison

**(1751-1836) Virginia**

James Madison did his homework! He came up with many of the ideas for the U.S. Constitution. He used the Virginia Constitution as a model. He pushed for a strong federal government.

Patrick Henry, the governor of Virginia, refused to attend the Constitutional Convention. He said, "I smell a rat!" Henry feared that a strong government would take too many rights from states and individuals.

# CHAPTER 3

# The Constitutional Convention

*Patrick Henry is famous for saying "Give me liberty, or give me death!" during the Revolutionary War.*

A date was set for a Constitutional Convention in Philadelphia. On May 14, 1787, delegates met to develop a plan for a new government. But only delegates from Virginia and Pennsylvania showed up on the right date.

Bad weather made travel slow and difficult. New Hampshire didn't have enough money for its delegates' trip. Others worried about the meeting's true purpose. Were leaders planning to take away states' rights?

Benjamin Franklin was not feeling well on the first day of the convention. He was carried to the meeting in a sedan chair.

Many Americans wanted George Washington to be king of the United States!

Slowly, delegates trickled in. The meeting finally started on May 25. Delegates decided to keep their discussions secret. Guards kept out the public and newpaper reporters. It was very hot inside, but the curtains and windows remained closed.

The delegates agreed that General George Washington should be president of the convention. He was known for his fairness. The delegates trusted him. They were ready to get to work!

George Washington led 55 leaders in creating a new constitution. The Constitutional Convention met from May to September of 1787.

# CHAPTER 4

# Working Out the Problems

 All delegates except James Madison skipped some of the convention's meetings.

America's leaders wanted a government that could protect people but would still give them their rights. It would have to be fair for all the states. There were many problems to solve. Disagreements among the delegates broke out almost immediately.

# Big Against Small

James Madison presented the Virginia Plan first. It called for three branches of government. The delegates agreed that one branch of government would have the power to pass laws. That branch was Congress. The problem was deciding how many representives in Congress to give to each state.

The Virginia Plan gave bigger states more representatives. Delegates from smaller states objected. They did not want big states to have more power. Smaller states supported William Paterson's New Jersey Plan. It called for every state to have the same number of representatives in Congress.

The original senators were all men. In 2006, there were 16 female senators.

Delegates argued for nearly seven weeks. Finally, Roger Sherman from Connecticut had a solution. Split Congress into two parts, called houses. Each state would get two representatives in one of the houses. This house would be the Senate. Bigger states would have more representatives in the other house, the House of Representatives.

On July 16, the agreement called the Great **Compromise** passed by a single vote. One problem was solved!

Today, the Senate still follows the rules of the Great Compromise: Each state has two senators.

# The Slavery Question

Another argument among the delegates was about slavery. Under the Virginia Plan, states with slaves got more representatives. Some delegates worried that states would get more slaves to gain representatives in Congress.

Slavery was still legal when the Constitution was written.

# Constitution Timeline

## 1776
Colonies declare independence on July 4.

## 1783
The Revolutionary War ends. The United States is free!

Some delegates at the convention tried to outlaw slavery. States with slavery fought to save it. The convention came to a halt.

Again, the only solution was a compromise. Slaves would count for less than other people. Every five slaves would count as three free people. This was called the Three-Fifths Compromise.

**1788**
**The ninth state, New Hampshire, approves the Constitution. It becomes law.**

**1789**
**The U.S. government begins operating under the Constitution.**

**1787**
**The Constitutional Convention takes place.**

# Getting to the Finish Line

Some delegates were not satisfied. They worried that the Constitution created powers only for the government. What about the rights of the people? What about the rights of the states?

Most delegates were hot, tired, and not ready for another argument. They voted "no" to adding a list of rights for people. They agreed to give Congress a way to change the Constitution in the future, however.

On September 17, 1787, the Constitution was ready. Benjamin Franklin asked that the document be approved by "unanimous consent of all states present." Thirty-nine delegates voted to accept the Constitution as written.

Three delegates refused to sign because the Constitution didn't protect people's rights. Others left early to avoid signing.

Delegates wait their turn to sign the Constitution. They used ink and quill pens, or feathers that were formed into pens.

The next step was for each state's government to approve the Constitution. Nine of the 13 states had to approve it. But there was a great deal of debate among the states, so this took more time.

Finally, in 1788, New Hampshire provided the ninth vote. The U.S. Constitution was now the law of the land.

On July 26, 1788, a parade in New York City celebrated the ratification of the Constitution.

# Inside the Constitution

The Constitution is just four pages long. It has an introduction, or **preamble**, and seven articles.

## The Preamble says:

*"We the People of the United States . . . "* are going to create a constitution.

Article 1 **creates the legislative, or lawmaking, branch — the Congress.**

Article 2 **creates the executive branch — the presidency.**

Article 3 **creates the judicial branch — the court system.**

Article 4 **explains the rights and powers of the states.**

Article 5 **explains how Congress may amend, or change, the Constitution.**

Article 6 **says the Constitution is the highest law of the land. It also states that people do not have to be religious to be elected.**

Article 7 **explains how the Constitution is to be approved. Once nine of the 13 states approved, it became law.**

The U.S. Constitution established the parts of government that stand today. Here, members of Congress and the Supreme Court justices gather to hear President George W. Bush's State of the Union speech, in 2005.

# CHAPTER 5

# The Constitution in Action

*An amendment was proposed in 1893 to rename the country the "United States of the Earth"!*

The U.S. Constitution is still the highest law in the land. It divides the government into three parts, or branches, so that no one part will become too powerful. This is known as "checks and balances." The Constitution gives each part some power over the other two. This document is the basis of our government today.

# THE THREE BRANCHES
# OF GOVERNMENT

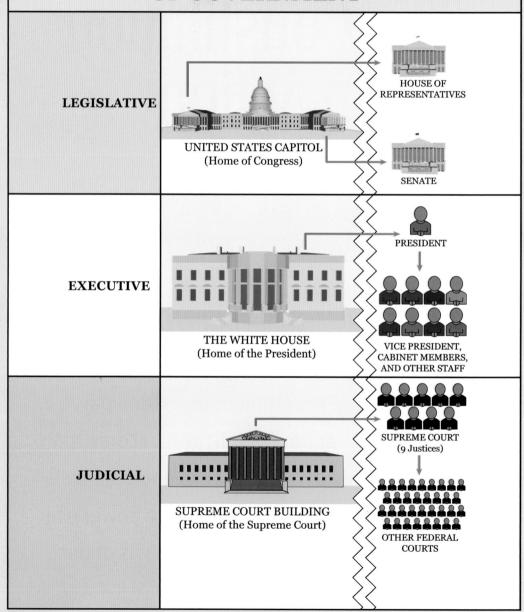

**LEGISLATIVE**

UNITED STATES CAPITOL
(Home of Congress)

HOUSE OF
REPRESENTATIVES

SENATE

**EXECUTIVE**

THE WHITE HOUSE
(Home of the President)

PRESIDENT

VICE PRESIDENT,
CABINET MEMBERS,
AND OTHER STAFF

**JUDICIAL**

SUPREME COURT BUILDING
(Home of the Supreme Court)

SUPREME COURT
(9 Justices)

OTHER FEDERAL
COURTS

# The Three Branches

The first three articles of the Constitution set up the federal government. The articles explain the duties of each branch of our government. Each branch has different powers.

The **legislative** branch has the power to make laws. This branch is the Congress. It includes the Senate and the House of Representatives. For a law to pass, more than half the members of each house need to vote for it.

The **executive** branch enforces laws. It is made up of a president, a vice president, and the president's staff.

The **judicial** branch makes sure that the laws are written and used correctly. The U.S. Supreme Court and other federal courts are part of this branch. The courts make sure that Congress and the president apply all laws fairly.

# The Document Grows

The framers of the Constitution gave the people the power to change things as the country changed. Congress can add **amendments** to the Constitution. At least two-thirds of each house of Congress must approve an amendment. Three-quarters of the states must also approve it.

Since 1788, there have been more than 9,000 proposed amendments. Only 27 have passed.

This illustration shows the celebration in the House of Representatives after the 13th Amendment abolished slavery in 1865.

# The Bill of Rights

The first 10 amendments are called the Bill of Rights. The states approved them in 1791. James Madison proposed these amendments to give people more protection from the government.

Connecticut, Georgia, and Massachusetts did not ratify the Bill of Rights until 1939.

The Bill of Rights protects all Americans. The rights include freedom of speech. That allows people to say and write what they think. The Bill of Rights promises Americans freedom of religion. It gives Americans the right to a trial by jury. That way, no one can be put in jail without a fair trial.

States proposed more than 200 amendments to create the Bill of Rights. The final version includes only 10.

# Other Amendments

Long after the Bill of Rights was approved, other important amendments were added. The 13th Amendment put an end to slavery in 1865. The 19th Amendment gave women the right to vote in 1920.

Only one amendment has ever been overturned. That's the 18th Amendment. It outlawed the use of alcohol in the United States. It was approved in 1919. It was overturned by the 21st Amendment in 1933.

The State of Mississippi did not ratify the 13th Amendment, to abolish slavery, until 1995.

**African Americans gained the right to vote soon after the 13th Amendment was passed. In 1870, this right became protected by the Constitution under the 15th Amendment.**

In 1920, the 19th Amendment gave women the right to vote. Here, women celebrate their victory in Washington, D.C.

## Still Going Strong

The original words that the delegates wrote in 1787 have never been changed. The founders recognized that their work was not perfect. Amendments have allowed the document to grow and change.

The Constitution was a blueprint for a nation that would last for years to come. More than 200 years later, the Constitution is still the highest law of the land. ★

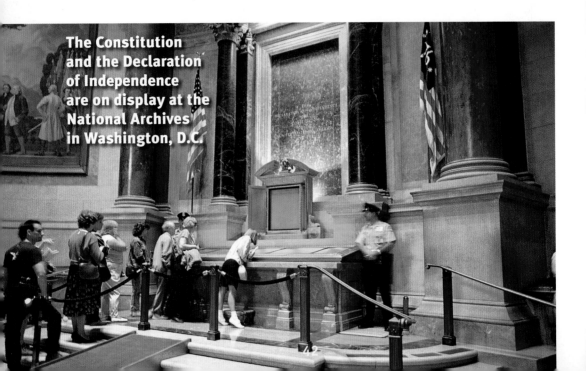

The Constitution and the Declaration of Independence are on display at the National Archives in Washington, D.C.

# True Statistics

**Approved on:** June 21, 1788

**Approved at:** Pennsylvania State House (now Independence Hall)

**Word count:** 4,543 words, including the signatures

**Days it took to write:** Fewer than 100

**Oldest person to sign:** Benjamin Franklin, 81

**Youngest person to sign:** New Jersey delegate Jonathan Dayton, age 26

**Amount a clerk was paid to write the final draft:** $30

**On display at:** National Archives, Washington, D.C.

**Year of the last amendment:** 1992

# Did you find the truth?

**F** The Constitution is made up of all the laws of the United States.

**T** The Constitution created the U.S. government of today.

# Resources

## Books

Collins, James Lincoln. *The Benjamin Franklin You Never Knew*. Danbury, CT: Children's Press, 2004.

Leebrick, Kristal. *The United States Constitution*. Mankato, MN: Bridgestone Books, 2002.

Maddex, Robert L. *The U.S. Constitution—A to Z*. Washington, DC: CQ Press, 2002.

Marcovitz, Hal. *The Constitution*. Philadelphia: Mason Crest Publishers, 2003.

Sobel, Syl. *The U.S. Constitution and You*. Hauppauge, NY: Barron's Educational Series, 2001.

Taylor-Butler, Christine. *The Bill of Rights*. Danbury, CT: Children's Press, 2008.

Travis, Cathy. *Constitution Translated for Kids*. Austin: Synergy Books, 2006.

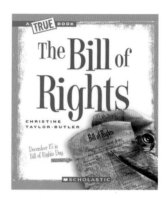

# Organizations and Web Sites

**The Constitution for Kids (for grades 4–7)**
www.usConstitution.net/constkids4.html
Find out more about the Constitution at this site for kids.

**Independence Hall Association**
www.ushistory.org
Learn more about other historic U.S. documents.

**National Constitution Center**
www.constitutioncenter.org
Check out this interactive information on the Constitution and its framers.

# Places to Visit

**National Archives**
700 Pennsylvania Avenue NW
Washington, DC 20408-0001
202-357-5000
www.archives.gov
Visit the Bill of Rights,
see letters from George
Washington, and more.

**The White House**
1600 Pennsylvania Avenue NW
Washington, DC 20500
202-456-2121
www.whitehouse.gov
See where the executive branch
of government does its work

# Important Words

**amendments** – changes or additions to a legal document

**compromise** – a solution that satisfies both sides

**congress** – a body of elected officials who meet to debate and pass laws

**constitution** (kon-stuh-TOO-shun) – a document that describes the basic laws and organization of a state or country

**delegates** – people chosen to represent others at a meeting

**executive** – related to the branch of government that enforces laws; the president is part of the executive branch

**federal** – relating to a form of government in which states are united under one central power

**judicial** (joo-DI-shuhl) – related to the branch of government that contains the court system, including the Supreme Court

**legislative** (le-juhs-LAY-tiv) – related to the branch of government that makes laws; Congress is the legislative branch

**preamble** (PREE-am-buhl) – the introductory part of a constitution that explains the reasons for and purposes of the laws

**Revolutionary War** – a war from 1775 to 1783 that gave the 13 American colonies independence from Great Britain

**unanimous** (yoo-NA-nuh-muhss) – having the agreement of all

# Index

# About the Author

Christine Taylor-Butler has written more than 30 books for children. She has written several books in the True Book American History series, including *The Bill of Rights*, *The Congress of the United States*, *The Supreme Court*, and *The Presidency*.

A native of Ohio, Taylor-Butler now lives in Kansas City, Missouri, with her husband, Ken, and their two daughters. She holds degrees in both civil engineering and art and design from the Massachusetts Institute of Technology.